Presented to:

Irene pas.llas

From:

ZONDERVAN

Celebrate Recovery Journal Updated Edition
Copyright ©2006 by John Baker

Requests for information should be addressed to:
Zondervan, *3900 Sparks Dr. SE, Grand Rapids, Michigan 49546*

ISBN 978-0-310-09034-2

Cover design: Brand Navigation
Cover photography: 123rf.com

First Printing May 2017 / Printed in the United States of America

JOHN BAKER

Celebrate
Recovery®

INTRODUCTION

By John Baker

Journaling—Starting a Healthy Habit!

In Celebrate Recovery we talk about our hurts, hang ups, and habits. We focus on the habits that have affected us and others in a negative way. We discovered that with God's healing grace and working the Celebrate Recovery program we can break the chains that the destructive habits have had on us. As we continue to grow in our recoveries, we also learn that there are some healthy habits that we need to start doing. The following are the positive habits we need to form if we are going to work our program successfully:

- Attending our Celebrate Recovery meetings regularly
- Talking to our sponsors and accountability partners
- Doing a daily inventory
- Getting into God's Word daily
- Having a daily quiet time
- Giving back by serving others

These are all positive habits! The best way to know how we are growing in recovery is to keep a daily journal; a daily record of our interaction with others, our feelings, our victories, and areas that we still need to improve.

Lamentations 3:40 exhorts us to "Let us examine our ways and test them, and let us return to the LORD."

If you haven't used a journal so far in your recovery, I believe you will find this recovery tool a great help! I encourage you to make journaling a daily habit, a daily part of your program.

It has been said that it takes 21 days to form a habit. Commit to giving journaling a three week try. Ask your accountability team to help hold you accountable. By the end of the third week you will discover that this is a necessary and helpful addition to your recovery program!

First Corinthians 10:12 puts it this way: "So, if you think you are standing firm, be careful that you don't fall!"

How to Get Started Journaling

Your journal is not for you to just record a recap of your daily schedule. It's not as much about "what" you did today as much as it is about "how" you did today. Your journal is a tool for you to review and write down your good and bad behaviors and what happened to you today.

In John 3:21 Jesus tells us, "Whoever lives by the truth comes into the light...." Journaling, on a daily basis, helps bring us into the light.

I know for many of you this may be the first experience in writing down your thoughts on a daily basis. It is important to recap your day in written form. Some of you may have trouble getting started. Let me give you three hints that will help you get started putting the ink on the paper:

1. Start out by writing down one thing that you are thankful for from your experiences from the day. Just that one thing will get you started and it will also help you sleep better that night.

2. Ask your accountability partner/sponsor to hold you accountable for writing in your journal every night.

3. This is the one that really works for me! Memorize Galatians 5:22–23, the "fruit of the Spirit": "The fruit of the Spirit is love, joy, peace, patience, kindness, goodness, faithfulness, gentleness and self-control."

Daily ask yourself any of these questions to prompt your writing, starting each question with the word "today":

- How did I show love to others?
- Did I act in an unloving way toward anyone?
- Did others see in me the joy of having a personal relationship with the Lord? If not, why not?

- How was my serenity, my peace? Did anything happen that caused me to lose it? What was my part in it?
- Was I patient? What caused me to lose my patience? Do I owe anyone amends?
- Would anyone say that I was kind/good? In what ways did I act unkind?
- How was my faithfulness? Did I keep my word with everyone?
- How was my gentleness and self-control? Did I lose my temper, speak a harsh or unkind word to someone?

Our goal in recovery is to humbly live each day—in reality, not denial. Through God's guidance, we can learn to make choices about the emotions that affect our thinking and actions. We start to take action—positive action—instead of constant reaction.

We desire to grow daily in our relationship with Jesus Christ and others. Instead of attempting to be in control of every situation and every person we come in contact with, or spinning out of control ourselves, we are starting to exhibit self-control, the way God wants us to be. Remember, self-control under God's control is what we are striving for. Journaling will help us stay on track.

Also, remember to keep your daily inventory, your journaling, balanced. Be sure to include the things that you did right throughout the day. It is important to write down even small victories. The best way to stay balanced is to journal.

Conduct a 90-Day Review of Your Journaling

Every three months, I get away on a "mini-retreat"! I would encourage you to try it. Bring your journal with you, and pray as you read through the last ninety days of your journal entries. Ask God to show you areas in your life that you can improve on in the next ninety days and celebrate the victories that you have made.

Look for negative patterns, issues that you are continually writing down and having to promptly make amends for—again and again. Share them with your sponsor or accountability partner, and set up an action plan for yourself, with God's help, to overcome them. With God's help we can keep our side of the street clean.

You will find "My 90-day Journal Review" sheets starting on page 238.

> "Search me, God, and know my heart;
>   test me and know my anxious thoughts.
> See if there is any offensive way in me,
>   and lead me in the way everlasting."
>
> PSALM 139:23-24

How to Use Your Prayer Journal

I n the last section of the journal, you will find several pages for you to use as your prayer journal. A prayer journal is simply writing down your prayer requests. It is divided into two sections – "Prayer Request" and "God's Answer."

> *"Do not be anxious about anything, but in every situation, by prayer and petition, with thanksgiving, present your requests to God. And the peace of God, which transcends all understanding, will guard your hearts and your minds in Christ Jesus."*
> PHILIPPIANS 4:6-7

> *"Keep on asking, and you will receive what you ask for."*
> MATTHEW 7:7 NLT

It is exciting to look back and review your prayer journal and see how faithful God has been in answering your prayers. Just remember, God will answer your prayers according to his purpose and plan for your life.

> *"And my God will meet all your needs according to the riches of his glory in Christ Jesus."*
> PHILIPPIANS 4:19

My Personal Journaling Journey

I would like to close the introduction to the Celebrate Recovery Journal by sharing some of the excerpts from my personal journal. These are just some of the "turning points" in my recovery journey. If I had not written them down I may have forgotten their impact on my life. It is my hope and prayer that they will help you see the great benefits in keeping a daily journal.

February 14, 1991 — Made my amends to my wife, Cheryl

I asked Cheryl to meet me for lunch today. I simply told her that she was not responsible for my drinking, and I was truly sorry for all the pain and heartache that I had caused in her life. I told her that I still loved her, and that if I could ever do anything for her—anything—all she had to do was ask. She graciously accepted my amends. I'm not sure what God has planned for us; however, we will be going on the journey together.

November 21, 1991 — First meeting of Celebrate Recovery at Saddleback

"WOW! Forty–three brave people came tonight. The band was great and the four small groups went well. Thank you, God. I was very nervous. I would like to say it was all the excitement, but I was filled with a lot of old fears and self-doubt. When I gave the talk in the large group time, my mouth was so dry that I could hardly talk. But we made it. The ministry is launched. After all we have been through, it's great that Cheryl and I can serve God together. I pray that God brings everyone back next week. I still can't believe or understand "why" God chose me to start "Celebrate Recovery."

December 23, 1991 — Argument with Laura, my daughter

"I blew it today. My daughter wanted to have her boyfriend join us for Christmas dinner. I said that I wanted our first Christmas that we were back together as a family to just be the four of us. We got into an argument. I now see that I was being selfish. I did not consider her feelings and my old friend 'pride' wouldn't let me back down. Just when I think that I'm growing in my recovery, I take a giant step back-wards. I owe Laura an amends. God help me stop slipping back to my old behaviors."

Note: I learned from my journal that for years I couldn't admit when I was wrong. I couldn't admit my mistakes. My refusal to offer amends blocked all my relationships, especially with my family. As I grew and matured in the Word and recovery, I discovered that I had to own my mistakes and take responsibility for my actions. I couldn't do that if I didn't take time daily to journal and allow God to show me where I missed the mark.

October 25, 2000 — My Dad's death

"What I remember most about my Dad was his gentleness. He was a true gentle-man. He was soft-spoken and very kind. He loved the Lord and the Word. When I was growing up, he would leave for work hours before my Mom and I got up. He would always have a hand-written Bible verse waiting for us to read at breakfast. He taught me, he didn't just tell me, how to live a Christ-centered life. He taught me, he didn't tell me, how to love your wife and children.

Through all the years that I struggled with my sin-addiction to alcohol, and through all the pain and heartache I caused, he never gave up on me. He truly showed me unconditional love. I will miss my model, my friend, my dad. But he was more than ready to go home. I thank God that he didn't have to suffer."

March 3, 2003 — Meeting with President Bush

"This has been a day that I will never forget! To think that four other recovery leaders and I would ever have a chance to sit down and share for 40 minutes with the President of the United States! What a gentleman. He really cares about those struggling with a hurt, hang up, or habit. In his speech after our meeting, he said, 'Then there's John Baker, the founder of Celebrate Recovery. Big John is with us.... He and I shared something in common.... We used to drink too much. And our hearts changed. And then we quit. That is a tried-and-true formula.'"

June 18, 2004 — Maggie, our first grandchild's birth

"Thank you God! What a gift. She's beautiful! Johnny and Jeni are going to be great parents. She's healthy and definitely a 'Maggie'. I pray that she has a life full of joy and peace, and that she loves and grows closer to her parents and You more every day. Please protect her and bless her. At Celebrate Recovery tonight, I was showing off her pictures.

Special Note: God blessed me with a second granddaughter, Chloe, who was born March 26, 2006.

One of my greatest joys is to know that my grandaughters will never see their Grandpa take a drink of alcohol. One of my greatest sorrows is that my kids saw me drink way too much."

Key Verses for Journaling

LAMENTATIONS 3:40

Let us examine our ways and test them, and let us return to the LORD.

1 CORINTHIANS 10:12

So, if you think you are standing firm, be careful that you don't fall!

JOHN 3:21

But whoever lives by the truth comes into the light, so that it may be seen plainly that what they have done has been done in the sight of God.

GALATIANS 5:22-23

The fruit of the Spirit is love, joy, peace, forbearance, kindness, goodness, faithfulness, gentleness and self-control...

PSALM 139:23-24

Search me, God, and know my heart; test me and know my anxious thoughts. See if there is any offensive way in me, and lead me in the way everlasting.

PHILIPPIANS 4:6-7

Do not be anxious about anything, but in every situation, by prayer and petition, with thanksgiving, present your requests to God. And the peace of God, which transcends all understanding, will guard your hearts and your minds in Christ Jesus.

MATTHEW 7:7 NLT

Keep on asking, and you will receive what you ask for.

PHILIPPIANS 4:19

And my God will meet all your needs according to the riches of his glory in Christ Jesus.

BY PASTOR RICK WARREN

1. Realize I'm not God. I admit that I am powerless to control my tendency to do the wrong thing and that my life is unmanageable.

     Happy are those who know they are spiritually poor.

2. Earnestly believe that God exists, that I matter to Him, and that He has the power to help me recover.

     Happy are those who mourn, for they shall be comforted.

3. Consciously choose to commit all my life and will to Christ's care and control.

     Happy are the meek.

4. Openly examine and confess my faults to myself, to God, and to someone I trust.

     Happy are the pure in heart.

5. Voluntarily submit to every change God wants to make in my life and humbly ask Him to remove my character defects.

     Happy are those whose greatest desire is to do what God requires.

6. Evaluate all my relationships. Offer forgiveness to those who have hurt me and make amends for harm I've done to others, except when to do so would harm them or others.

     Happy are the merciful. Happy are the peacemakers.

7. Reserve a daily time with God for self-examination, Bible reading, and prayer in order to know God and His will for my life and to gain the power to follow His will.

8. Yield myself to God to be used to bring this Good News to others, both by my example and by my words

     Happy are those who are persecuted because they do what God requires.

TWELVE STEPS AND THEIR BIBLICAL COMPARISONS[1]

1. We admitted we were powerless over our addictions and compulsive behaviors. That our lives had become unmanageable.

   "For I know that good itself does not dwell in me, that is, in my sinful nature. For I have the desire to do what is good, but I cannot carry it out." (Romans 7:18)

2. Came to believe that a power greater than ourselves could restore us to sanity.

   "For it is God who works in you to will and to act in order to fulfill his good purpose." (Philippians 2:13)

3. Made a decision to turn our lives and our wills over to the care of God.

   "Therefore, I urge you, brothers and sisters, in view of God's mercy, to offer your bodies as a living sacrifice, holy and pleasing to God—this is your true and proper worship." (Romans 12:1)

4. Made a searching and fearless moral inventory of ourselves.

   "Let us examine our ways and test them, and let us return to the LORD." (Lamentations 3:40)

5. Admitted to God, to ourselves, and to another human being the exact nature of our wrongs.

   "Therefore confess your sins to each other and pray for each other so that you may be healed." (James 5:16)

6. Were entirely ready to have God remove all these defects of character.

   "Humble yourselves before the Lord, and he will lift you up." (James 4:10)

7. Humbly asked Him to remove all our shortcomings.

    "If we confess our sins, he is faithful and just and will forgive us our sins and purify us from all unrighteousness." (1 John 1:9)

8. Made a list of all persons we had harmed and became willing to make amends to them all.

    "Do to others as you would have them do to you." (Luke 6:31)

9. Made direct amends to such people whenever possible, except when to do so would injure them or others.

    "Therefore, if you are offering your gift at the altar and there remember that your brother or sister has something against you, leave your gift there in front of the altar. First go and be reconciled to them; then come and offer your gift." (Matthew 5:23–24)

10. Continued to take personal inventory and when we were wrong, promptly admitted it.

    "So, if you think you are standing firm, be careful that you don't fall!" (1 Corinthians 10:12)

11. Sought through prayer and meditation to improve our conscious contact with God, praying only for knowledge of His will for us and power to carry that out.

    "Let the message of Christ dwell among you richly." (Colossians 3:16)

12. Having had a spiritual experience as the result of these steps, we tried to carry this message to others, and practice these principles in all our affairs.

    "Brothers and sisters, if someone is caught in a sin, you who live by the Spirit should restore that person gently. But watch yourselves, or you also may be tempted." (Galatians 6:1)

1. Throughout this material, you will notice several references to the Christ-centered 12 Steps. Our prayer is that Celebrate Recovery will create a bridge to the millions of people who are familiar with the secular 12 Steps (I acknowledge the use of some material from the 12 Suggested Steps of Alcoholics Anonymous) and in so doing, introduce them to the one and only true Higher Power, Jesus Christ. Once they begin that relationship, asking Christ into their hearts as Lord and Savior, true healing and recovery can begin!

PRAYER FOR SERENITY

God, grant me the serenity

to accept the things I cannot change,

the courage to change the things I can,

and the wisdom to know the difference.

Living one day at a time,

enjoying one moment at a time;

accepting hardship as a pathway to peace;

taking, as Jesus did,

this sinful world as it is,

not as I would have it;

trusting that You will make all things right

if I surrender to Your will;

so that I may be reasonably happy in this life

and supremely happy with You forever in the next.

Amen.

REINHOLD NIEBUHR

PRINCIPLE 1

REALIZE I'M NOT GOD. I ADMIT THAT I AM
POWERLESS TO CONTROL MY TENDENCY TO
DO THE WRONG THING AND THAT MY
LIFE IS UNMANAGEABLE.

Happy are those who know they are spiritually poor.
MATTHEW 5:3 GNT

Dear God, Your Word tells me that I can't heal my hurts, hang-ups, and habits by just saying that they are not there. Help me! Parts of my life, or all of my life, are out of control. I now know that I cannot "fix" myself. It seems the harder that I try to do the right thing, the more I struggle. Lord, I want to step out of my denial and into the truth. I pray for You to show me the way. In Your Son's name, amen.

PRINCIPLE 1 ~ Realize I'm not God. I admit that I am powerless to control my tendency to do the wrong thing and that my life is unmanageable.

For I know that good itself does not dwell in me, that is, in my sinful nature.
For I have the desire to do what is good, but I cannot carry it out.

_____

_____

_____

_____

_____

_____

_____

_____

_____

> *You can't heal a wound by
> saying it's not there!*
>
> JEREMIAH 6:14 TLB

_____

_____

_____

_____

_____

_____

_____

_____

_____

> *They promise them freedom while they themselves are slaves of destructive habits—for we are slaves of anything that has conquered us.*
>
> 2 PETER 2:19 GNT

PRINCIPLE I ~ Realize I'm not God. I admit that I am powerless to control my tendency to do the wrong thing and that my life is unmanageable.

_____

_____

_____

_____

_____

_____

_____

_____

_____

_____

_____

_____

_____

_____

_____

_____

_____

_____

_____

He frees the prisoners...; he lifts the burdens
from those bent down beneath their loads.
PSALM 146:7–8 TLB

PRINCIPLE 1 ~ Realize I'm not God. I admit that I am powerless to control my tendency to do the wrong thing and that my life is unmanageable.

_____

_____

_____

_____

_____

_____

_____

_____

_____

_____

_____

_____

_____

_____

_____

_____

_____

_____

They cried to the Lord in their troubles, and he rescued them! He led them
from the darkness and shadow of death and snapped their chains.

PSALM 107:13–14 TLB

_____

_____

_____

_____

_____

_____

_____

_____

> *God is light; in him there is no darkness at all. If we claim to have fellowship with him yet walk in the darkness, we lie and do not live out the truth. But if we walk in the light, as he is in the light, we have fellowship with one another, and the blood of Jesus, his Son, purifies us from all sin.*
>
> 1 JOHN 1:5–7

_____

_____

_____

_____

_____

_____

> *Stop lying to each other;*
> *tell the truth, for we are*
> *parts of each other and when*
> *we lie to each other we are*
> *hurting ourselves.*
>
> EPHESIANS 4:25 TLB

PRINCIPLE I ~ Realize I'm not God. I admit that I am powerless to control my tendency to do the wrong thing and that my life is unmanageable.

God's promise: "I will give you back your health again
and heal your wounds."
JEREMIAH 30:17 TLB

PRINCIPLE I ~ Realize I'm not God. I admit that I am powerless to control my tendency to do the wrong thing and that my life is unmanageable.

_____

_____

_____

_____

_____

_____

_____

_____

_____

_____

_____

_____

_____

_____

_____

Pride ends in a fall, while humility brings honor.
PROVERBS 29:23 TLB

> *Jesus said, "Whatever is covered up will be uncovered, and every secret will be made known. So then, whatever you have said in the dark will be heard in broad daylight."*
>
> LUKE 12:2–3 GNT

> Jesus said, "So don't be anxious about tomorrow. God will take care of your tomorrow too. Live one day at a time."
>
> MATTHEW 6:34 TLB

PRINCIPLE I ~ Realize I'm not God. I admit that I am powerless to control my tendency to do the wrong thing and that my life is unmanageable.

_____

_____

_____

_____

_____

_____

_____

_____

_____

_____

_____

_____

_____

_____

_____

_____

_____

For light is capable of "showing up" everything for what it really is. It is even possible (after all, it happened to you!) for light to turn the thing it shines upon into light also.

EPHESIANS 5:13–14 PHILLIPS

PRINCIPLE 1 ~ Realize I'm not God. I admit that I am powerless to control my tendency to do the wrong thing and that my life is unmanageable.

_____

_____

_____

_____

_____

_____

_____

_____

_____

_____

_____

_____

_____

_____

_____

_____

_____

In your anger do not sin: Do not let the sun go down while you are still
angry, and do not give the devil a foothold.
EPHESIANS 4:26–27

_____

_____

_____

_____

_____

_____

_____

> *Continue to love each other with true brotherly love. Don't forget to be kind to strangers, for some who have done this have entertained angels without realizing it!*
>
> HEBREWS 13:1–2 TLB

_____

_____

_____

_____

_____

_____

_____

_____

_____

> *Jesus said, "My purpose is to give life in all its fullness."*
>
> <small>JOHN 10:10 TLB</small>

PRINCIPLE I ~ Realize I'm not God. I admit that I am powerless to control my tendency to do the wrong thing and that my life is unmanageable.

_____

_____

_____

_____

_____

_____

_____

_____

_____

_____

_____

_____

_____

_____

_____

_____

_____

Jesus said, "Whoever clings to his life shall lose it,
and whoever loses his life shall save it."
LUKE 17:33 TLB

PRINCIPLE 1 ~ Realize I'm not God. I admit that I am powerless to control my tendency to do the wrong thing and that my life is unmanageable.

_____

_____

_____

_____

_____

_____

_____

_____

_____

_____

_____

_____

_____

_____

_____

_____

_____

I am convinced that nothing can ever separate us from his love. Death can't,
and life can't. The angels won't, and all the powers of hell itself cannot keep
God's love away.... Nothing will ever be able to separate us from the love of
God demonstrated by our Lord Jesus Christ when he died for us.
ROMANS 8:38–39 TLB

_____

_____

_____

_____

_____

_____

_____

_____

_____

_____

_____

_____

> *Pity me, O Lord, for I am weak. Heal me, for my body is sick, and I am upset and disturbed. My mind is filled with apprehension and with gloom.*
>
> PSALM 6:2–3 TLB

_____

_____

_____

_____

_____

_____

_____

_____

_____

_____

_____

> Jesus said, "You cannot be a slave of two masters; you will hate one and love the other; you will be loyal to one and despise the other."
>
> MATTHEW 6:24 GNT

PRINCIPLE I ~ Realize I'm not God. I admit that I am powerless to control my tendency to do the wrong thing and that my life is unmanageable.

_____

_____

_____

_____

_____

_____

_____

_____

_____

_____

_____

_____

_____

_____

_____

_____

_____

_____

_____

_____

_____

_____

Jesus said, "With man this is impossible, but with God all things are possible."
MATTHEW 19:26

PRINCIPLE I ~ Realize I'm not God. I admit that I am powerless to control my tendency to do the wrong thing and that my life is unmanageable.

_____

_____

_____

_____

_____

_____

_____

_____

_____

_____

_____

_____

_____

_____

_____

_____

_____

_____

Problems far too big for me to solve are piled higher than my head.
Meanwhile my sins, too many to count, have all caught up with me
and I am ashamed to look up.
PSALM 40:12 TLB

> *If you wait for perfect conditions, you will never get anything done.*
>
> ECCLESIASTES 11:4 TLB

> *My heart is troubled and restless. Waves of affliction have come upon me.*
>
> JOB 30:27 TLB

PRINCIPLE I ~ Realize I'm not God. I admit that I am powerless to control my tendency to do the wrong thing and that my life is unmanageable.

I don't understand myself at all, for I really want to do what is right, but I can't.
I do what I don't want to—what I hate. I know perfectly well that what I am
doing is wrong, and my bad conscience proves that I agree with these laws I am
breaking. But I can't help myself, because I'm no longer doing it. It is sin inside
me that is stronger than I am that makes me do these evil things.

ROMANS 7:15–17 TLB

PRINCIPLE 1 ~ Realize I'm not God. I admit that I am powerless to control my tendency to do the wrong thing and that my life is unmanageable.

_Before every man there lies a wide and pleasant road
that seems right but ends in death._

PROVERBS 14:12 TLB

> *My good days are in the past.*
> *My hopes have disappeared.*
> *My heart's desires are broken.*
>
> JOB 17:11 TLB

> *I am worn out with pain;*
> *every night my pillow is*
> *wet with tears. My eyes are*
> *growing old and dim with*
> *grief because of all*
> *my enemies.*
>
> PSALM 6:6–7 TLB

PRINCIPLE

Principle 2

Earnestly believe that God exists, that I matter to Him, and that He has the power to help me recover.

Happy are those who mourn; God will comfort them!
Matthew 5:4 GNT

Dear God, I have tried to "fix" and "control" my life's hurts, hang-ups, or habits all by myself. I admit that, by myself, I am powerless to change. I need to begin to believe and receive Your power to help me recover. You loved me enough to send Your Son to the cross to die for my sins. Help me be open to the hope that I can only find in Him. Please help me to start living my life one day at a time. In Jesus' name I pray, amen.

PRINCIPLE 2 ~ Earnestly believe that God exists, that I matter to Him, and that He has the power to help me recover.

_____

_____

_____

_____

_____

_____

_____

_____

_____

_____

_____

_____

_____

_____

_____

_____

_____

_____

Anyone who comes to [God] must believe that he exists and that
he rewards those who earnestly seek him.

HEBREWS 11:6

> *You, my soul, find*
> *rest in God;*
> *my hope comes from him.*
>
> PSALM 62:5

> *Everything comes from God alone. Everything lives by his power.*
>
> ROMANS 11:36 TLB

PRINCIPLE 2 ~ Earnestly believe that God exists, that I matter to Him, and that He has the power to help me recover.

_____

_____

_____

_____

_____

_____

_____

_____

_____

_____

_____

_____

_____

_____

_____

_____

_____

_____

_____

My grace is enough for you: for where there is weakness,
my power is shown the more completely.
2 CORINTHIANS 12:9 PHILLIPS

PRINCIPLE 2 ~ Earnestly believe that God exists, that I matter to Him, and that He has the power to help me recover.

Now your attitudes and thoughts must all be constantly changing for the better.... You must be a new and different person.

EPHESIANS 4:23 TLB

_____

_____

_____

_____

_____

_____

_____

_____

> *For I can do everything God asks me to with the help of Christ who gives me the strength and power.*
>
> PHILIPPIANS 4:13 TLB

_____

_____

_____

_____

_____

_____

_____

_____

_____

_____

> *Lead me; teach me;*
> *for you are the God who*
> *gives me salvation. I have no*
> *hope except in you.*
>
> PSALM 25:5 TLB

PRINCIPLE 2 ~ Earnestly believe that God exists, that I matter to Him, and that He has the power to help me recover.

I am sure that God who began the good work within you will keep right on helping you grow in his grace until his task within you is finally finished on that day when Jesus Christ returns.

PHILIPPIANS 1:6 TLB

PRINCIPLE 2 ~ Earnestly believe that God exists, that I matter to Him, and that He has the power to help me recover.

_____

_____

_____

_____

_____

_____

_____

_____

_____

_____

_____

_____

_____

_____

_____

_____

_____

_____

_____

*Jesus said, "For if you had faith even as small as a tiny mustard seed
you could say to this mountain, 'Move!' and it would go far away.
Nothing would be impossible."*
MATTHEW 17:20 TLB

_____

_____

_____

_____

_____

_____

_____

_____

_____

_____

_____

_____

_____

_____

> *If you declare with your mouth, "Jesus is Lord," and believe in your heart that God raised him from the dead, you will be saved.*
>
> ROMANS 10:9

_____

_____

_____

_____

_____

_____

_____

_____

_____

_____

> *God is our refuge and strength, an ever-present help in trouble. Therefore we will not fear.*
>
> PSALM 46:1–2

PRINCIPLE 2 ~ Earnestly believe that God exists, that I matter to Him, and that He has the power to help me recover.

My mind and my body may grow weak, but God is my strength;
he is all I ever need.

PSALM 73:26 GNT

PRINCIPLE 2 ~ Earnestly believe that God exists, that I matter to Him, and that He has the power to help me recover.

Accept one another, then, for the glory of God, as Christ has accepted you.
ROMANS 15:7 GNT

PRINCIPLE

_____

_____

_____

_____

_____

_____

_____

_____

_____

_____

_____

_____

_____

_____

_____

_____

_____

> *We were really crushed and overwhelmed, and feared we would never live through it. We felt we were doomed to die and saw how powerless we were to help ourselves; but that was good, for then we put everything into the hands of God. [God] ... alone could save us ... and we expect him to do it again and again.*
>
> 2 CORINTHIANS 1:8–10 TLB

_____

_____

_____

_____

_____

> *Nothing gives me greater joy than to hear that my children are following the way of truth.*
>
> 3 John v. 4 NCV

PRINCIPLE 2 ~ Earnestly believe that God exists, that I matter to Him, and that He has the power to help me recover.

_____

_____

_____

_____

_____

_____

_____

_____

_____

_____

_____

_____

_____

_____

_____

_____

_____

_____

It is dangerous to be concerned with what others think of you,
but if you trust the LORD, you are safe.
PROVERBS 29:25 GNT

PRINCIPLE 2 ~ Earnestly believe that God exists, that I matter to Him, and that He has the power to help me recover.

_____

_____

_____

_____

_____

_____

_____

_____

_____

_____

_____

_____

_____

_____

_____

_____

_____

_____

While we were still sinners, Christ died for us.
ROMANS 5:8

_____

_____

_____

_____

_____

_____

_____

_____

> *And God is faithful; he will not let you be tempted beyond what you can bear. But when you are tempted, he will also provide a way out.*
>
> 1 CORINTHIANS 10:13

_____

_____

_____

_____

_____

_____

_____

_____

_____

> *Praise be to the Lord, to God our Savior, who daily bears our burdens.*
>
> PSALM 68:19

PRINCIPLE 2 ~ Earnestly believe that God exists, that I matter to Him, and that He has the power to help me recover.

_____

_____

_____

_____

_____

_____

_____

_____

_____

_____

_____

_____

_____

_____

_____

_____

_____

_____

_____

The LORD is good, a refuge in times of trouble.
He cares for those who trust in him.
NAHUM 1:7

PRINCIPLE 2 ~ Earnestly believe that God exists, that I matter to Him, and that He has the power to help me recover.

_____

_____

_____

_____

_____

_____

_____

_____

_____

_____

_____

_____

_____

_____

_____

_____

_____

_____

_____

_____

_____

_____

Jesus said, " So don't be anxious about tomorrow.
God will take care of your tomorrow too. Live one day at a time."
MATTHEW 6:34 TLB

Remember that in the past you were without Christ. You were not citizens of Israel, and you had no part in the agreements with the promise that God made to his people. You had no hope, and you did not know God. But now in Christ Jesus, you who were far away from God are brought near through the blood of Christ's death.

> *But this precious treasure—this light and power that now shine within us—is held in a perishable container, that is, in our weak bodies. Everyone can see that the glorious power within must be from God and is not our own. We are pressed on every side by troubles, but not crushed and broken. We are perplexed because we don't know why things happen as they do, but we don't give up and quit.*
>
> 2 CORINTHIANS 4:7–8 TLB

PRINCIPLE 2 ~ Earnestly believe that God exists, that I matter to Him, and that He has the power to help me recover.

And this is the secret: Christ in your hearts is your only hope of glory.
COLOSSIANS 1:27 TLB

PRINCIPLE 2 ~ Earnestly believe that God exists, that I matter to Him, and that He has the power to help me recover.

_____

_____

_____

_____

_____

_____

_____

_____

_____

_____

_____

_____

_____

_____

_____

_____

_____

_____

_____

_____

Don't copy the behavior and customs of this world, but be a new and different person with a fresh newness in all you do and think. Then you will learn from your own experience how his ways will really satisfy you.
ROMANS 12:2 TLB

_____

_____

_____

_____

_____

_____

_____

_____

_____

_____

_____

_____

> *He will not break the bruised reed, nor quench the dimly burning flame. He will encourage the fainthearted, those tempted to despair. He will see full justice given to all who have been wronged.*
>
> ISAIAH 42:3 TLB

_____

_____

_____

_____

_____

_____

_____

_____

PRINCIPLE 2 ~ Earnestly believe that God exists, that I matter to Him, and that He has the power to help me recover.

_____

_____

_____

_____

_____

_____

_____

_____

_____

_____

_____

_____

_____

_____

_____

_____

_____

_____

For it is God who works in you to will and to act
in order to fulfill his good purpose.
PHILIPPIANS 2:13

PRINCIPLE 3

CONSCIOUSLY CHOOSE TO COMMIT ALL MY LIFE AND WILL TO CHRIST'S CARE AND CONTROL.

Happy are those who are humble.
MATTHEW 5:5 GNT

Dear God, I have tried to do it all by myself, on my own power, and I have failed. Today, I want to turn my life over to You. I ask You to be my Lord and my Savior. You are the One and only Higher Power! I ask that You help me start to think less about me and my will . It is my prayer to daily turn my will over to you, to daily seek Your direction and wisdom for my life. Please continue to help me overcome my hurts, hang-ups, and habits and may that victory over them help others as they see Your power at work in changing my life. It is my prayer to do Your will always. In Jesus' name I pray, amen.

PRINCIPLE 3 ~ Consciously choose to commit all my life and will to Christ's care and control.

If you declare with your mouth, "Jesus is Lord," and believe in your heart that God raised him from the dead, you will be saved.

ROMANS 10:9

Trust in the LORD with all your heart and lean not on your own understanding; in all your ways submit to him, and he will make your paths straight.

PROVERBS 3:5–6

> *Jesus said, "Turn from your sins and act on this glorious news!"*
>
> MARK 1:15 TLB

PRINCIPLE 3 - Consciously choose to commit all my life and will to Christ's care and control.

_____

_____

_____

_____

_____

_____

_____

_____

_____

_____

_____

_____

_____

_____

_____

_____

Don't let the world around you squeeze you into its own mould, but let God re-mould your minds from within, so that you may prove in practice that the plan of God for you is good, meets all his demands and moves towards the goals of true maturity.

ROMANS 12:2 PHILLIPS

PRINCIPLE 3- Consciously choose to commit all my life and will to Christ's care and control.

_____

_____

_____

_____

_____

_____

_____

_____

_____

_____

_____

_____

_____

_____

_____

_____

_____

Now God says he will accept and acquit us—declare us "not guilty"—if we trust Jesus Christ to take away our sins.

ROMANS 3:22 TLB

Teach me to do your will,
for you are my God;
may your good Spirit
lead me on level ground.

PSALM 143:10

> Jesus said, "Come to me and I will give you rest—all of you who work so hard beneath a heavy yoke. Wear my yoke—for it fits perfectly—and let me teach you; for I am gentle and humble, and you shall find rest for your souls."
>
> MATTHEW 11:28–30 TLB

PRINCIPLE 3 ~ Consciously choose to commit all my life and will to Christ's care and control.

_____

_____

_____

_____

_____

_____

_____

_____

_____

_____

_____

_____

_____

_____

_____

_____

_____

_____

_____

_____

_____

*God who began the good work within you will keep right on helping you
grow in his grace until his task within you is finally finished.*
PHILIPPIANS 1:6 TLB

_____

_____

_____

_____

_____

_____

_____

_____

_____

_____

_____

_____

_____

_____

_____

_____

_____

_____

_____

Jesus said, "So don't be anxious about tomorrow. God will take care of your tomorrow too. Live one day at a time."
MATTHEW 6:34 TLB

> "Because of your little faith," Jesus told them. "For if you had faith even as small as a tiny mustard seed you could say to this mountain, 'Move!' and it would go far away. Nothing would be impossible."
>
> MATTHEW 17:20 TLB

> *Commit everything you do to the Lord. Trust him to help you do it and he will.*
>
> PSALM 37:5 TLB

PRINCIPLE 3 ~ Consciously choose to commit all my life and will to Christ's care and control.

Lead me; teach me; for you are the God who gives me salvation.
I have no hope except in you.
PSALM 25:5 TLB

_____

_____

_____

_____

_____

_____

_____

_____

_____

_____

_____

_____

_____

_____

_____

_____

_____

Indeed, we felt we had received the sentence of death. But this happened that we might not rely on ourselves but on God, who raises the dead.

2 CORINTHIANS 1:9

_____

_____

_____

_____

_____

_____

_____

_____

_____

_____

_____   > *In everything you do, put*
                                            > *God first, and he will direct*
_____   > *you and crown your efforts*
                                            > *with success.*
_____
                                            > PROVERBS 3:6 TLB
_____

_____

_____

_____

_____

_____

_____

_____

_____

_____

_____

> *Therefore, I urge you, brothers and sisters, in view of God's mercy, to offer your bodies as a living sacrifice, holy and pleasing to God—this is your true and proper worship.*
>
> ROMANS 12:1

PRINCIPLE 4

OPENLY EXAMINE AND CONFESS MY FAULTS TO
MYSELF, TO GOD, AND TO SOMEONE I TRUST.

Happy are the pure in heart.
MATTHEW 5:8 GNT

Dear God, You know my past, all the good and the bad things
that I've done. In this step, I ask that You give me the strength
and the courage to list those things so that I can "come clean"
and face them and the truth. Please help me reach out to
others You have placed along my "road to recovery." Thank
You for providing them to help me keep balanced as I do my
inventory. In Christ's name I pray, amen.

PRINCIPLE 4 ~ Openly examine and confess my faults to myself, to God, and to someone I trust.

_____

_____

_____

_____

_____

_____

_____

_____

_____

_____

_____

_____

_____

_____

_____

_____

_____

_____

_____

_____

_____

_____

_____

Then listen to me. Keep silence and I will teach you wisdom!

JOB 33:33 TLB

PRINCIPLE

_____

_____

_____

_____

_____

_____

_____

_____

_____

_____

> *Let me express my anguish.*
> *Let me be free to speak out of*
> *the bitterness of my soul.*
>
> JOB 7:11 TLB

_____

_____

_____

_____

_____

_____

_____

> *Love the Lord, all of you who are his people; for the Lord protects those who are loyal to him.... So cheer up! Take courage if you are depending on the Lord.*
>
> PSALM 31:23–24 TLB

PRINCIPLE 4 - Openly examine and confess my faults to myself,
to God, and to someone I trust.

_____

_____

_____

_____

_____

_____

_____

_____

_____

_____

_____

_____

_____

_____

_____

_____

_____

_____

_____

_____

_____

The LORD gave us mind and conscience; we cannot hide from ourselves.
PROVERBS 20:27 GNT

PRINCIPLE 4 - Openly examine and confess my faults to myself, to God, and to someone I trust.

_____

_____

_____

_____

_____

_____

_____

_____

_____

_____

_____

_____

_____

_____

_____

_____

_____

Let us examine our ways and test them.

LAMENTATIONS 3:40

_____

_____

_____

_____

_____

_____

_____

_____

> *Two are better off than one,*
> *because together they can*
> *work more effectively. If one*
> *of them falls down, the other*
> *can help him up. But if some-*
> *one is alone ... there is no one*
> *to help him.... Two people can*
> *resist an attack that would*
> *defeat one person alone.*
>
> ECCLESIASTES 4:9–10, 12 GNT

_____

_____

_____

_____

_____

_____

_____

> *As iron sharpens iron, so one person sharpens another.*
>
> PROVERBS 27:17

PRINCIPLE 4 ~ Openly examine and confess my faults to myself, to God, and to someone I trust.

_____

_____

_____

_____

_____

_____

_____

_____

_____

_____

_____

_____

_____

_____

_____

_____

_____

_____

_____

Get rid of all bitterness, rage and anger, brawling and slander,
along with every form of malice.
EPHESIANS 4:31

PRINCIPLE 4 - Openly examine and confess my faults to myself, to God, and to someone I trust.

_____

_____

_____

_____

_____

_____

_____

_____

_____

_____

_____

_____

_____

_____

_____

_____

_____

_____

Fear not, for I am with you. Do not be dismayed. I am your God.
I will strengthen you; I will help you; I will uphold you
with my victorious right hand.

ISAIAH 41:10 TLB

_____

_____

_____

_____

_____

_____

_____

_____

_____

_____

_____

> *I will look for those that are lost, bring back those that wander off, bandage those that are hurt, and heal those that are sick.*
>
> EZEKIEL 34:16 GNT

_____

_____

_____

_____

_____

_____

_____

_____

> *Examine me, O God, and know my mind; test me, and discover ... if there is any evil in me and guide me in the everlasting way.*
>
> PSALM 139:23–24 GNT

PRINCIPLE 4 - Openly examine and confess my faults to myself, to God, and to someone I trust.

_____

_____

_____

_____

_____

_____

_____

_____

_____

_____

_____

_____

_____

_____

_____

_____

_____

_____

_____

"Come, let's talk this over!" says the Lord; "no matter how deep the stain of your sins, I can take it out and make you as clean as freshly fallen snow. Even if you are stained as red as crimson, I can make you white as wool!"

ISAIAH 1:18 TLB

PRINCIPLE 4 ~ Openly examine and confess my faults to myself, to God, and to someone I trust.

Jesus said, "Forgive us our sins, just as we have forgiven those who have sinned against us. Don't bring us into temptation, but deliver us from the Evil One."
MATTHEW 6:12–13 TLB

He will give them to you
if you give him first place
in your life and live as he
wants you to.

MATTHEW 6:33 TLB

> Get rid of all bitterness,
> passion, and anger. No more
> shouting or insults, no more
> hateful feelings of any sort.
>
> EPHESIANS 4:31 GNT

PRINCIPLE 4 - Openly examine and confess my faults to myself, to God, and to someone I trust.

_____

_____

_____

_____

_____

_____

_____

_____

_____

_____

_____

_____

_____

_____

_____

_____

_____

_____

_____

_____

_____

Do not lie to each other. You have left your old sinful life
and the things you did before.
COLOSSIANS 3:9 NCV

PRINCIPLE 4 - Openly examine and confess my faults to myself, to God, and to someone I trust.

_____

_____

_____

_____

_____

_____

_____

_____

_____

_____

_____

_____

_____

_____

_____

_____

Search me, O God, and know my heart; test my thoughts.
Point out anything you find in me that makes you sad,
and lead me along the path of everlasting life.
PSALM 139:23–24 TLB

> *Do not conform any longer to the pattern of this world, but be transformed by the renewing of your mind. Then you will be able to test and approve what God's will is—his good, pleasing and perfect will.*
>
> ROMANS 12:2

> *Haven't you yet learned that your body is the home of the Holy Spirit God gave you, and that he lives within you? Your own body does not belong to you. For God has bought you with a great price. So use every part of your body to give glory back to God, because he owns it.*
>
> 1 CORINTHIANS 6:19–20 TLB

PRINCIPLE 4 - Openly examine and confess my faults to myself, to God, and to someone I trust.

_____

_____

_____

_____

_____

_____

_____

_____

_____

_____

_____

_____

_____

_____

_____

_____

_____

But if you are unwilling to obey the Lord, then decide today whom you will obey.... But as for me and my family, we will serve the Lord.

JOSHUA 24:15 TLB

Let us not neglect our church meetings, as some people do,
but encourage and warn each other, especially now that the day
of his coming back again is drawing near.

HEBREWS 10:25 TLB

Jesus said,
"I am with you always."

MATTHEW 28:20 TLB

> *All who are oppressed may come to him. He is a refuge for them in their times of trouble.*
>
> PSALM 9:9 TLB

PRINCIPLE 4 ~ Openly examine and confess my faults to myself, to God, and to someone I trust.

Yes, be bold and strong! Banish fear and doubt! For remember, the Lord your God is with you wherever you go.

JOSHUA 1:9 TLB

_Let him have all your worries and cares, for he is always thinking
about you and watching everything that concerns you._

1 PETER 5:7 TLB

> *Whoever conceals their sins*
> *does not prosper,*
> *but the one who confesses and*
> *renounces them finds mercy.*
>
> PROVERBS 28:13

> "As surely as I am the living God," says the Lord, "everyone will kneel before me, and everyone will confess that I am God." Every one of us, then, will have to give an account to God.
>
> ROMANS 14:11–12 GNT

PRINCIPLE 4 - Openly examine and confess my faults to myself, to God, and to someone I trust.

_____

_____

_____

_____

_____

_____

_____

_____

_____

_____

_____

_____

_____

_____

_____

_____

Therefore confess your sins to each other and pray for each other
so that you may be healed.
JAMES 5:16

PRINCIPLE 4 - Openly examine and confess my faults to myself, to God, and to someone I trust.

_All have sinned; ... yet now God declares us "not guilty" ...
if we trust in Jesus Christ, who ... freely takes away our sins._
ROMANS 3:23–24 TLB

_____

_____

_____

_____

_____

_____

_____

_____

_____

> *Jesus said,*
> *"I am the light of the world.*
> *Whoever follows me*
> *will never walk in darkness,*
> *but will have*
> *the light of life."*
>
> JOHN 8:12

_____

_____

_____

_____

_____

_____

_____

_____

_____

Jesus said, "Then you will know the truth, and the truth will set you free."

JOHN 8:32

PRINCIPLE 4 - Openly examine and confess my faults to myself, to God, and to someone I trust.

_____

_____

_____

_____

_____

_____

_____

_____

_____

_____

_____

_____

_____

_____

There was a time when I wouldn't admit what a sinner I was. But my dishonesty made me miserable and filled my days with frustration.... My strength evaporated like water on a sunny day until I finally admitted all my sins to you and stopped trying to hide them. I said to myself, "I will confess them to the Lord." And you forgave me! All my guilt is gone.

PSALM 32:3–5 TLB

PRINCIPLE 4 - Openly examine and confess my faults to myself, to God, and to someone I trust.

_____

_____

_____

_____

_____

_____

_____

_____

_____

_____

_____

_____

_____

_____

_____

_____

_____

Jesus said, "Why do you look at the speck of sawdust in your brother's eye and fail to notice the plank in your own? How can you say to your brother, 'Let me get the speck out of your eye,' when there is a plank in your own?... Take the plank out of your own eye first, and then you can see clearly enough to remove your brother's speck of dust."

MATTHEW 7:3 PHILLIPS

PRINCIPLE

For God was in Christ,
restoring the world to
himself, no longer counting
men's sins against them
but blotting them out.

2 CORINTHIANS 5:19 TLB

> "Let us examine our ways and test them, and let us return to the LORD."
>
> LAMENTATIONS 3:40

PRINCIPLE 5

VOLUNTARILY SUBMIT TO EVERY CHANGE GOD
WANTS TO MAKE IN MY LIFE AND HUMBLY ASK
HIM TO REMOVE MY CHARACTER DEFECTS.

*Happy are those whose greatest desire is to do what
God requires.*
MATTHEW 5:6 GNT

Dear God, thank You for taking me this far in my recovery journey.
Now I pray for Your help in making me be entirely ready to change
all my shortcomings. Give me the strength to deal with all of my
character defects that I have turned over to You. Allow me to accept all the changes that You want to make in me. Help me be the
person that You want me to be. In Your Son's name I pray, amen.

PRINCIPLE 5 - Voluntarily submit to every change God wants to make in my life and humbly ask Him to remove my character defects.

_____

_____

_____

_____

_____

_____

_____

_____

_____

_____

_____

_____

_____

_____

_____

_____

_____

Help me to do your will, for you are my God. Lead me in good paths,
for your Spirit is good.
PSALM 143:10 TLB

> *Commit everything you do to the Lord. Trust him to help you do it and he will.*
>
> PSALM 37:5 TLB

So then, have your minds ready for action. Keep alert and set your hope completely on the blessing which will be given you when Jesus Christ is revealed. Be obedient to God, and do not allow your lives to be shaped by those desires you had when you were still ignorant.

1 PETER 1:13–14 GNT

PRINCIPLE

PRINCIPLE 5 -Voluntarily submit to every change God wants to make in my life and humbly ask Him to remove my character defects.

_____

_____

_____

_____

_____

_____

_____

_____

_____

_____

_____

_____

_____

_____

_____

_____

_____

_____

_____

When an evil spirit goes out of a person, it travels over dry country looking for a place to rest. If it can't find one, it says to itself, 'I will go back to my house.' So it goes back and finds the house empty, ... then it goes out and brings along seven other spirits even worse than itself, and they come and live there.
MATTHEW 12:43–45 GNT

PRINCIPLE 5 -Voluntarily submit to every change God wants to make in my life and humbly ask Him to remove my character defects.

_____

_____

_____

_____

_____

_____

_____

_____

_____

_____

_____

_____

_____

_____

_____

_____

_____

_____

_____

The person who has been born into God's family does not make a practice of sinning, because now God's life is in him; so he can't keep on sinning, for this new life has been born into him and controls him—he has been born again.

1 JOHN 3:9 TLB

> *He has given us more and more strength to stand against such evil longings. As the Scripture says, God gives strength to the humble, but sets himself against the proud and haughty. So give yourselves humbly to God. Resist the devil and he will flee from you.*
>
> JAMES 4:6–7 TLB

> *So get rid of all that is wrong in your life, both inside and outside, and humbly be glad for the wonderful message we have received, for it is able to save our souls as it takes hold of our hearts.*
>
> JAMES 1:21 TLB

PRINCIPLE 5 -Voluntarily submit to every change God wants to make in my life and humbly ask Him to remove my character defects.

_____

_____

_____

_____

_____

_____

_____

_____

_____

_____

_____

_____

_____

_____

_____

_____

_____

For I can never forget these awful years; always my soul will live in utter shame. Yet there is one ray of hope: his compassion never ends. It is only the Lord's mercies that have kept us from complete destruction.

LAMENTATIONS 3:20–22 TLB

PRINCIPLE 5 -Voluntarily submit to every change God wants to make in my life and humbly ask Him to remove my character defects.

_____

_____

_____

_____

_____

_____

_____

_____

_____

_____

_____

_____

_____

_____

_____

_____

_____

_____

_____

*O loving and kind God, have mercy. Have pity upon me and
take away the awful stain of my transgressions. Oh, wash me, cleanse me
from this guilt. Let me be pure again.*
PSALM 51:1—2 TLB

_____

_____

_____

_____

_____

_____

_____

> *If we confess our sins, he is faithful and just and will forgive us our sins and purify us from all unrighteousness.*
>
> 1 JOHN 1:9

_____

_____

_____

_____

_____

_____

_____

_____

> *Offer yourselves as a living sacrifice to God, dedicated to his service and pleasing to him.... Let God transform you inwardly by a complete change of your mind.*
>
> ROMANS 12:1–2 GNT

PRINCIPLE 5 -Voluntarily submit to every change God wants to make in my life and humbly ask Him to remove my character defects.

_____

_____

_____

_____

_____

_____

_____

_____

_____

_____

_____

_____

_____

_____

_____

_____

_____

_____

_____

In their hearts humans plan their course,
but the LORD *determines their steps.*
PROVERBS 16:9

PRINCIPLE 5 -Voluntarily submit to every change God wants to make in my life and humbly ask Him to remove my character defects.

_____

_____

_____

_____

_____

_____

_____

_____

_____

_____

_____

_____

_____

_____

_____

_____

When you draw close to God, God will draw close to you.
Wash your hands, you sinners, and let your hearts be filled
with God alone to make them pure and true to him.
JAMES 4:8 TLB

_____

_____

_____

_____

_____

_____

_____

_____

> *The Lord is faithful, and*
> *he will strengthen you and*
> *protect you from the evil one.*
>
> 2 THESSALONIANS 3:3

_____

_____

_____

_____

_____

_____

_____

_____

_____

> *Now glory be to God who by his mighty power at work within us is able to do far more than we would ever dare to ask or even dream of — infinitely beyond our highest prayers, desires, thoughts, or hopes.*
>
> EPHESIANS 3:20 TLB

PRINCIPLE 5 -Voluntarily submit to every change God wants to make in my life and humbly ask Him to remove my character defects.

_____

_____

_____

_____

_____

_____

_____

_____

_____

_____

_____

_____

_____

_____

_____

_____

_____

_____

And I am sure that God who began the good work within you will keep right on helping you grow in his grace until his task within you is finally finished on that day when Jesus Christ returns.

PHILIPPIANS 1:6 TLB

PRINCIPLE 5 -Voluntarily submit to every change God wants to make in my life and humbly ask Him to remove my character defects.

_____

_____

_____

_____

_____

_____

_____

_____

_____

_____

_____

_____

_____

_____

_____

_____

_____

_____

God gives strength to the humble ... so give yourselves humbly to God.
Resist the devil and he will flee from you. And when you draw close to God,
God will draw close to you.

JAMES 4:6–8 TLB

_____

_____

_____

_____

_____

_____

_____

_____

> *If you want to know what
> God wants you to do, ask
> him, and he will gladly tell
> you, for he is always ready
> to give a bountiful supply of
> wisdom to all who ask him;
> he will not resent it.*
>
> JAMES 1:5 TLB

_____

_____

_____

_____

_____

_____

_____

> *Let us examine our ways and test them, and let us return to the LORD."*
>
> LAMENTATIONS 3:40

PRINCIPLE 6

EVALUATE ALL MY RELATIONSHIPS. OFFER FORGIVE-
NESS TO THOSE WHO HAVE HURT ME AND MAKE
AMENDS FOR HARM I'VE DONE TO OTHERS, EXCEPT
WHEN TO DO SO WOULD HARM THEM OR OTHERS.

Happy are those who are merciful.
MATTHEW 5:7 GNT

Happy are those who work for peace.
MATTHEW 5:9 GNT

Dear God, thank You for Your love, for Your freely given grace. Help me model your ways when I make my amends to those I have hurt and offer my forgiveness to those who have injured me. Help me to set aside my selfishness and speak the truth in love. I pray that I would focus only on my part, my responsibility in the issue. I know that I can forgive others because You first forgave me. Thank You for loving me. In Jesus' name I pray, amen.

PRINCIPLE 6 ~ Evaluate all my relationships. Offer forgiveness to those who have hurt me and make amends for harm I've done to others, except when to do so would harm them or others.

_____

_____

_____

_____

_____

_____

_____

_____

_____

_____

_____

_____

_____

_____

_____

_____

_____

_____

_____

_____

_____

Jesus said, "Do not judge others, and God will not judge you; do not condemn others, and God will not condemn you; forgive others, and God will forgive you."

LUKE 6:37 GNT

Jesus said, "Treat others as you want them to treat you."

LUKE 6:31 TLB

> *And let us consider how we may spur one another on toward love and good deeds.*
>
> HEBREWS 10:24

PRINCIPLE 6 ~ Evaluate all my relationships. Offer forgiveness to those who have hurt me and make amends for harm I've done to others, except when to do so would harm them or others.

_____

_____

_____

_____

_____

_____

_____

_____

_____

_____

_____

_____

_____

_____

_____

_____

Jesus said, "Love your enemies and do good to them;
lend and expect nothing back."
LUKE 6:35 GNT

PRINCIPLE 6 ~ Evaluate all my relationships. Offer forgiveness to those who have hurt me and make amends for harm I've done to others, except when to do so would harm them or others.

Value others above yourselves, not looking to your own interests,

but each of you to the interests of others.

PHILIPPIANS 2:3–4

Jesus said, "Therefore, if you are offering your gift at the altar and there remember that your brother or sister has something against you, leave your gift there in front of the altar. First go and be reconciled to them; then come and offer your gift."
MATTHEW 5:23–24

> *Jesus said, "It is finished."*
>
> JOHN 19:30

PRINCIPLE 6 ~ Evaluate all my relationships. Offer forgiveness to those who have hurt me and make amends for harm I've done to others, except when to do so would harm them or others.

_____

_____

_____

_____

_____

_____

_____

_____

_____

_____

_____

_____

_____

God puts people right through their faith in Jesus Christ. God does this to all who believe in Christ, because there is no difference at all: everyone has sinned and is far away from God's saving presence. But by the free gift of God's grace all are put right with him through Christ Jesus, who sets them free. God offered him, so that by his blood he should become the means by which people's sins are forgiven through their faith in him.

ROMANS 3:22–25 GNT

PRINCIPLE 6 ~ Evaluate all my relationships. Offer forgiveness to those who have hurt me and make amends for harm I've done to others, except when to do so would harm them or others.

_____

_____

_____

_____

_____

_____

_____

_____

_____

_____

_____

_____

_____

_____

_____

_____

_____

_____

_____

_____

Do not repay anyone evil for evil. Be careful to do what is right in the eyes of everyone. If it is possible, as far as it depends on you, live at peace with everyone.

ROMANS 12:17–18

After you have borne these suferings a very little while, God himself (from whom we receive all grace and has called you to share his eternal splendour through Christ) will himself make you whole and secure and strong.

1 PETER 5:10 PHILLIPS

> *Be gentle and ready to forgive; never hold grudges. Remember, the Lord forgave you, so you must forgive others.*
>
> COLOSSIANS 3:13 TLB

PRINCIPLE 6 ~ Evaluate all my relationships. Offer forgiveness to those who have hurt me and make amends for harm I've done to others, except when to do so would harm them or others.

_____

_____

_____

_____

_____

_____

_____

_____

_____

_____

_____

_____

_____

_____

_____

_____

_____

_____

_____

_____

You, therefore, have no excuse, you who pass judgment on someone else, for at whatever point you judge another, you are condemning yourself, because you who pass judgment do the same things.

ROMANS 2:1

PRINCIPLE 6 ~ Evaluate all my relationships. Offer forgiveness to those who have hurt me and make amends for harm I've done to others, except when to do so would harm them or others.

_____

_____

_____

_____

_____

_____

_____

_____

_____

_____

_____

_____

_____

_____

_____

_____

_____

_____

Jesus said, "Do not judge, and you will not be judged. Do not condemn, and you will not be condemned. Forgive, and you will be forgiven."

LUKE 6:37

Jesus said, "... and forgive us our sins, just as we have forgiven those who have sinned against us."

MATTHEW 6:12 TLB

> *So what should we say about this? If God is for us, no one can defeat us.*
>
> ROMANS 8:31 NCV

PRINCIPLE 6 ~ Evaluate all my relationships. Offer forgiveness to those who have hurt me and make amends for harm I've done to others, except when to do so would harm them or others.

_____

_____

_____

_____

_____

_____

_____

_____

_____

_____

_____

_____

_____

_____

_____

_____

_____

_____

_____

Jesus said, "My grace is enough for you. When you are weak, my power is made perfect in you." So I am very happy to brag about my weaknesses. Then Christ's power can live in me. For this reason I am happy when I have weaknesses, insults, hard times, sufferings, and all kinds of troubles for Christ. Because when I am weak, then I am truly strong.

2 CORINTHIANS 12:9–10 NCV

PRINCIPLE 6 ~ Evaluate all my relationships. Offer forgiveness to those who have hurt me and make amends for harm I've done to others, except when to do so would harm them or others.

_____

_____

_____

_____

_____

_____

_____

_____

_____

_____

_____

_____

_____

_____

_____

_____

_____

_____

_____

_____

All need to be made right with God by his grace, which is a free gift. They need to be made free from sin through Jesus Christ.

> *Prepare your minds for service and have self-control. All your hope should be for the gift of grace that will be yours when Jesus Christ is shown to you.*
>
> 1 PETER 1:13 NCV

> *For it is by grace you have been saved, through faith—and this not from yourselves, it is the gift of God—not by works, so that no one can boast.*
>
> EPHESIANS 2:8–9

_____

_____

_____

_____

_____

_____

_____

_____

_____

_____

_____

_____

_____

_____

_____

_____

_____

_____

_____

*Through whom we have gained access by faith into this grace in which we
now stand. And we rejoice in the hope of the glory of God.*

ROMANS 5:2

PRINCIPLE 6 ~ Evaluate all my relationships. Offer forgiveness to those who have hurt me and make amends for harm I've done to others, except when to do so would harm them or others.

Let us, then, feel very sure that we can come before God's throne where there is grace. There we can receive mercy and grace to help us when we need it.

Hebrews 4:16 NCV

> *Jesus said, "Forgive us our debts, as we also have forgiven our debtors."*
>
> MATTHEW 6:12

> *Jesus said, "If you forgive other people when they sin against you, your heavenly Father will also forgive you."*
>
> MATTHEW 6:14

PRINCIPLE 6 ~ Evaluate all my relationships. Offer forgiveness to those who have hurt me and make amends for harm I've done to others, except when to do so would harm them or others.

_____

_____

_____

_____

_____

_____

_____

_____

_____

_____

_____

_____

_____

_____

_____

_____

_____

I do not set aside the grace of God, for if righteousness could be gained through the law, Christ died for nothing!

GALATIANS 2:21

PRINCIPLE 6 ~ Evaluate all my relationships. Offer forgiveness to those who have hurt me and make amends for harm I've done to others, except when to do so would harm them or others.

_____

_____

_____

_____

_____

_____

_____

_____

_____

_____

_____

_____

_____

_____

_____

_____

_____

_____

In Christ we are set free by the blood of his death,
and so we have forgiveness of sins. How rich is God's grace.
EPHESIANS 1:7 NCV

_And I am sure that God who
began the good work within
you will keep right on helping
you grow in his grace until
his task within you is finally
finished on that day when
Jesus Christ returns._

PHILIPPIANS 1:6 TLB

> *May our Lord Jesus Christ himself and God our Father encourage you and strengthen you in every good thing you do and say. God loved us, and through his grace he gave us a good hope and encouragement that continues forever.*
>
> 2 THESSALONIANS 2:16 NCV

PRINCIPLE 6 ~ Evaluate all my relationships. Offer forgiveness to those who have hurt me and make amends for harm I've done to others, except when to do so would harm them or others.

_____

_____

_____

_____

_____

_____

_____

_____

_____

_____

_____

_____

_____

_____

_____

_____

_____

_____

If anyone says "I love God," but keeps on hating his brother, he is a liar; for if he doesn't love his brother who is right there in front of him, how can he love God whom he has never seen?

I JOHN 4:20 TLB

PRINCIPLE 6 ~ Evaluate all my relationships. Offer forgiveness to those who have hurt me and make amends for harm I've done to others, except when to do so would harm them or others.

_____

_____

_____

_____

_____

_____

_____

_____

_____

_____

_____

_____

_____

_____

_____

_____

_____

_____

Jesus said, "Love your enemies! Do good to them! Lend to them! And don't be concerned about the fact that they won't repay. Then your reward from heaven will be very great, and you will truly be acting as sons of God: for he is kind to the unthankful and to those who are very wicked."
LUKE 6:35 TLB

_____

_____

_____

_____

_____

_____

_____

> *Jesus said, "There is a saying,*
> *'Love your friends and hate*
> *your enemies.' But I say:*
> *Love your enemies! Pray for*
> *those who persecute you!"*
>
> MATTHEW 5:43–44 TLB

_____

_____

_____

_____

_____

_____

_____

_____

_____

> Never pay back evil for evil.
> Do things in such a way that
> everyone can see you are
> honest clear through. Don't
> quarrel with anyone. Be at
> peace with everyone, just as
> much as possible.
>
> ROMANS 12:17–18 TLB

PRINCIPLE 6 ~ Evaluate all my relationships. Offer forgiveness to those who have hurt me and make amends for harm I've done to others, except when to do so would harm them or others.

_____

_____

_____

_____

_____

_____

_____

_____

_____

_____

_____

_____

_____

_____

_____

_____

_____

Pay all your debts except the debt of love for others—never finish paying that! For if you love them, you will be obeying all of God's laws, fulfilling all his requirements.

ROMANS 13:8 TLB

PRINCIPLE 6 ~ Evaluate all my relationships. Offer forgiveness to those who have hurt me and make amends for harm I've done to others, except when to do so would harm them or others.

_____

_____

_____

_____

_____

_____

_____

_____

_____

_____

_____

_____

_____

_____

_____

_____

_____

_____

_____

Jesus said, "Do to others as you would have them do to you."

LUKE 6:31

PRINCIPLE 7

RESERVE A DAILY TIME WITH GOD FOR SELF-
EXAMINATION, BIBLE READING, AND PRAYER IN
ORDER TO KNOW GOD AND HIS WILL FOR MY LIFE
AND TO GAIN THE POWER TO FOLLOW HIS WILL.

Dear God, thank You for today. Thank You for giving me the tools to work my program and live my life differently, centered in Your will. Lord, help me to make my amends promptly and ask for forgiveness. In all my relationships today, help me to do my part in making them healthy and growing. In Jesus' name I pray, amen.

PRINCIPLE 7 ~ Reserve a daily time with God for self-examination, Bible reading, and prayer in order to know God and His will for my life and to gain the power to follow His will.

_____

_____

_____

_____

_____

_____

_____

_____

_____

_____

_____

_____

_____

_____

_____

_____

Jesus said, "If you live as I tell you to ... you will know the truth,
and the truth will set you free."
JOHN 8:32 TLB

> *If we say that we have no sin,*
> *we are only fooling ourselves,*
> *and refusing to accept the*
> *truth.... We are lying and*
> *calling God a liar, for he says*
> *we have sinned.*
>
> 1 JOHN 1:8–10 TLB

> Jesus said, "This is how I want you to conduct yourself in these matters. If you enter your place of worship and, about to make an offering, you suddenly remember a grudge a friend has against you, abandon your offering, leave immediately, go to this friend and make things right. Then and only then, come back and work things out with God."
>
> MATTHEW 5:23–24
> THE MESSAGE

PRINCIPLE 7 ~ Reserve a daily time with God for self-examination, Bible reading, and prayer in order to know God and His will for my life and to gain the power to follow His will.

_____

_____

_____

_____

_____

_____

_____

_____

_____

_____

_____

_____

_____

_____

_____

_____

_____

_____

_____

_____

Jesus said, "'Love the Lord your God with all your heart and ... soul and ... mind.' This is the first and greatest commandment. And the second is like it: 'Love your neighbor as yourself.' All the Law and the Prophets hang on these two commandments."

MATTHEW 22:37–40

PRINCIPLE 7 ~ Reserve a daily time with God for self-examination, Bible reading, and prayer in order to know God and His will for my life and to gain the power to follow His will.

_____

_____

_____

_____

_____

_____

_____

_____

_____

_____

_____

_____

_____

_____

_____

_____

_____

_____

_____

_____

Do not merely listen to the word, and so deceive yourselves. Do what it says.

JAMES 1:22

_____

_____

_____

_____

_____

_____

_____

_____

> *Our very lives were further proof to you of the truth of our message.*
>
> 1 THESSALONIANS 1:5 TLB

_____

_____

_____

_____

_____

_____

_____

_____

> *Intelligent people think before they speak; what they say is then more persuasive.*
>
> PROVERBS 16:23 GNT

PRINCIPLE 7 ~ Reserve a daily time with God for self-examination, Bible reading, and prayer in order to know God and His will for my life and to gain the power to follow His will.

_____

_____

_____

_____

_____

_____

_____

_____

_____

_____

_____

_____

_____

_____

_____

_____

_____

_____

_____

_____

_____

_____

*Do not let unwholesome [foul, profane, worthless, vulgar] words
ever come out of your mouth, but only such speech as is good
for building up others, according to the need and the occasion,
so that it will be a blessing to those who hear [you speak].*

EPHESIANS 4:29 AMP

_____

_____

_____

_____

_____

_____

_____

_____

_____

_____

_____

_____

_____

_____

_____

_____

_____

A wise, mature person is known for his understanding.
The more pleasant his words, the more persuasive he is.

PROVERBS 16:21 GNT

_A word of encouragement
does wonders!_

PROVERBS 12:25 TLB

> *If I had the gift of being able to speak in other languages without learning them, and could speak in every language there is in all of heaven and earth, but didn't love others, I would only be making noise.*
>
> 1 CORINTHIANS 13:1 TLB

PRINCIPLE 7 ~ Reserve a daily time with God for self-examination,
Bible reading, and prayer in order to know God and His will for
my life and to gain the power to follow His will.

_____

_____

_____

_____

_____

_____

_____

_____

_____

_____

_____

_____

_____

_____

_____

_____

Jesus said, "Watch and pray so that you will not fall into temptation.
The spirit is willing, but the body is weak."
MARK 14:38

PRINCIPLE 7 ~ Reserve a daily time with God for self-examination, Bible reading, and prayer in order to know God and His will for my life and to gain the power to follow His will.

_____

_____

_____

_____

_____

_____

_____

_____

_____

_____

_____

_____

_____

_____

_____

Be honest in your estimate of yourselves.... Hate what is wrong. Stand on the side of the good. Love each other.... Be patient in trouble.... Do things in such a way that everyone can see you are honest clear through.
ROMANS 12:3, 9–10, 12, 17 TLB

Test everything that is said to be sure it is true, and if it is, then accept it.

1 THESSALONIANS 5:21 TLB

> *Let everyone be sure that*
> *he is doing his very best, for*
> *then he will have the personal*
> *satisfaction of work well done,*
> *and won't need to compare*
> *himself with someone else.*
>
> GALATIANS 6:4 TLB

PRINCIPLE 7 ~ Reserve a daily time with God for self-examination, Bible reading, and prayer in order to know God and His will for my life and to gain the power to follow His will.

_____

_____

_____

_____

_____

_____

_____

_____

_____

_____

_____

_____

_____

_____

_____

_____

_____

Listen to the Lord. Hear what he is telling you!

ISAIAH 1:10 TLB

PRINCIPLE 7 ~ Reserve a daily time with God for self-examination, Bible reading, and prayer in order to know God and His will for my life and to gain the power to follow His will.

Be still, and know that I am God.
PSALM 46:10

_Don't worry about anything;
instead, pray about everything; tell God your needs
and don't forget to thank him
for his answers._

PHILIPPIANS 4:6 TLB

> *Listen to me. Keep silence and I will teach you wisdom!*
>
> JOB 33:33 TLB

PRINCIPLE 7 ~ Reserve a daily time with God for self-examination, Bible reading, and prayer in order to know God and His will for my life and to gain the power to follow His will.

_____

_____

_____

_____

_____

_____

_____

_____

_____

_____

_____

_____

_____

_____

_____

_____

_____

_____

If you do this you will experience God's peace, which is far more wonderful than the human mind can understand. His peace will keep your thoughts and your hearts quiet and at rest as you trust in Christ Jesus.

PHILIPPIANS 4:7 TLB

PRINCIPLE 7 ~ Reserve a daily time with God for self-examination, Bible reading, and prayer in order to know God and His will for my life and to gain the power to follow His will.

_____

_____

_____

_____

_____

_____

_____

_____

_____

_____

_____

_____

_____

_____

_____

_____

_____

Be joyful always, pray at all times, be thankful in all circumstances. This is what God wants from you in your life in union with Christ Jesus.

1 THESSALONIANS 5:16–18 GNT

Do not be anxious about anything, but in every situation, by prayer and petition, with thanksgiving, present your requests to God.

PHILIPPIANS 4:6

> *Let them give thanks to the
> LORD for his unfailing love
> and his wonderful deeds
> for mankind.*
>
> PSALM 107:15

PRINCIPLE 7 ~ Reserve a daily time with God for self-examination, Bible reading, and prayer in order to know God and His will for my life and to gain the power to follow His will.

_____

_____

_____

_____

_____

_____

_____

_____

_____

_____

_____

_____

_____

_____

_____

_____

_____

_____

Let the peace of Christ keep you in tune with each other, in step with each other. None of this going off and doing your own thing. And cultivate thankfulness. Let the Word of Christ—the Message—have the run of the house.

COLOSSIANS 3:15–16 THE MESSAGE

_____

_____

_____

_____

_____

_____

_____

_____

_____

_____

_____

_____

_____

_____

_____

_____

_____

_____

As for us, we have this large crowd of witnesses around us. So then, let us rid ourselves of everything that gets in the way, and the sin which holds on to us so tightly, and let us run with determination the race that lies before us.

HEBREWS 12:1 GNT

> *Enter the Temple gates*
> *with thanksgiving.*
>
> PSALM 100:4 GNT

> *The whole Bible was given to us by inspiration from God and is useful to teach us what is true and to make us realize what is wrong in our lives; it straightens us out and helps us do what is right.*
>
> 2 TIMOTHY 3:16 TLB

PRINCIPLE 7 ~ Reserve a daily time with God for self-examination, Bible reading, and prayer in order to know God and His will for my life and to gain the power to follow His will.

_____

_____

_____

_____

_____

_____

_____

_____

_____

_____

_____

_____

_____

_____

_____

_____

_____

_____

_____

Now your attitudes and thoughts must all be constantly changing for the better.

EPHESIANS 4:23 TLB

PRINCIPLE 7 ~ Reserve a daily time with God for self-examination, Bible reading, and prayer in order to know God and His will for my life and to gain the power to follow His will.

Job, listen to this: Stop and notice God's miracles.

JOB 37:14 NCV

_____

_____

_____

_____

_____

_____

_____

_____

_____

_____

_____

> *And if you leave God's paths and go astray, you will hear a Voice behind you say, "No, this is the way; walk here."*
>
> ISAIAH 30:21 TLB

_____

_____

_____

_____

_____

_____

_____

_____

_____

> *Oh, the joys of those who do not follow evil men's advice, who do not hang around with sinners, scoffing at the things of God: But they delight in doing everything God wants them to, and day and night are always meditating on his laws and thinking about ways to follow him more closely.*
>
> PSALM 1:1–2 TLB

PRINCIPLE 7 ~ Reserve a daily time with God for self-examination, Bible reading, and prayer in order to know God and His will for my life and to gain the power to follow His will.

_____

_____

_____

_____

_____

_____

_____

_____

_____

_____

_____

_____

_____

_____

_____

_____

_____

So now you can look forward soberly and intelligently to more of God's kindness to you when Jesus Christ returns. Obey God because you are his children; don't slip back into your old ways—doing evil because you knew no better.

1 PETER 1:13–14 TLB

PRINCIPLE 7 ~ Reserve a daily time with God for self-examination, Bible reading, and prayer in order to know God and His will for my life and to gain the power to follow His will.

Watch your step. Stick to the path and be safe. Don't sidetrack;
pull back your foot from danger.
PROVERBS 4:26–27 TLB

_____

_____

_____

_____

_____

_____

_____

_____

> *Jesus said, "Watch with me and pray lest the Tempter overpower you. For though the spirit is willing enough, the body is weak."*
>
> MARK 14:38 TLB

_____

_____

_____

_____

_____

_____

_____

_____

_____

> *So, if you think you are standing firm, be careful that you don't fall!*
>
> 1 CORINTHIANS 10:12

PRINCIPLE 8

YIELD MYSELF TO GOD TO BE USED TO BRING THIS
GOOD NEWS TO OTHERS, BOTH BY MY EXAMPLE
AND BY MY WORDS.

*Happy are those who are persecuted because
they do what God requires.*
MATTHEW 5:10 GNT

Dear Jesus, as it would please You, bring me someone today

whom I can serve. Amen.

PRINCIPLE 8 ~ Yield myself to God to be used to bring this Good News to others, both by my example and by my words.

Jesus said, "Freely you have received, freely give."
MATTHEW 10:8

> *[God] did not even keep back his own Son, but offered him for us all! He gave us his Son—will he not also freely give us all things?*
>
> ROMANS 8:32 GNT

> Jesus said, "You cannot
> serve two masters: God and
> money. For you will hate one
> and love the other, or else the
> other way around."
>
> MATTHEW 6:24 TLB

PRINCIPLE 8 ~ Yield myself to God to be used to bring this Good News to others, both by my example and by my words.

_____

_____

_____

_____

_____

_____

_____

_____

_____

_____

_____

_____

_____

_____

_____

_____

_____

_____

_____

_____

Jesus said, "'Love the Lord your God with all your heart and with all your soul and with all your mind.' This is the first and greatest commandment. And the second is like it: 'Love your neighbor as yourself.'"

MATTHEW 22:37–39

PRINCIPLE 8 ~ Yield myself to God to be used to bring this Good News to others, both by my example and by my words.

Two are better off than one, because together they can work more effectively. If one of them falls down, the other can help him up. But if someone is alone ... there is no one to help him.... Two people can resist an attack that would defeat one person alone.

ECCLESIASTES 4:9–12 GNT

> *Let us give thanks to the God and Father of our Lord Jesus Christ, the merciful Father, the God from whom all help comes! He helps us in all our troubles, so that we are able to help others who have all kinds of troubles, using the same help that we ourselves have received from God.*
>
> 2 CORINTHIANS 1:3–4 GNT

> *My children, our love should not be just words and talk; it must be true love, which shows itself in action.*
>
> 1 John 3:18 GNT

PRINCIPLE 8 ~ Yield myself to God to be used to bring this Good News to others, both by my example and by my words.

_____

_____

_____

_____

_____

_____

_____

_____

_____

_____

_____

_____

No one lights a lamp and then covers it with a washtub or shoves it under the bed. No, you set it up on a lamp stand so those who enter the room can see their way.... We're not hiding things; we're bringing everything out into the open. So be careful that you don't become misers.... Generosity begets generosity. Stinginess impoverishes.

LUKE 8:16–18 THE MESSAGE

PRINCIPLE 8 ~ Yield myself to God to be used to bring this Good News to others, both by my example and by my words.

_____

_____

_____

_____

_____

_____

_____

_____

_____

_____

_____

_____

_____

_____

_____

_____

If a Christian is overcome by some sin ... humbly help him back onto the right path, remembering that next time it might be one of you who is in the wrong. Share each other's troubles and problems, and so obey our Lord's command.

GALATIANS 6:1–2 TLB

_____

_____

_____

_____

_____

_____

_____

_____

_____

_____

> *Arouse the love that comes*
> *from a pure heart,*
> *a clear conscience,*
> *and a genuine faith.*
>
> 1 TIMOTHY 1:5 GNT

_____

_____

_____

_____

_____

_____

_____

_____

_____

_____

> Let us not love with
> words or speech but with
> actions and in truth.
>
> 1 JOHN 3:18

PRINCIPLE 8 ~ Yield myself to God to be used to bring this
Good News to others, both by my example and by my words.

_____

_____

_____

_____

_____

_____

_____

_____

_____

_____

_____

_____

_____

_____

_____

_____

_____

_____

*Jesus said, "Since I, the Lord and Teacher, have washed your feet,
you ought to wash each other's feet. I have given you an example to follow:
do as I have done to you."*

JOHN 13:14–15 TLB

PRINCIPLE 8 ~ Yield myself to God to be used to bring this Good News to others, both by my example and by my words.

What a wonderful God we have— he is the Father of our Lord Jesus Christ, the source of every mercy, and the one who so wonderfully comforts and strengthens us in our hardships and trials. And why does he do this? So that when others are troubled, needing our sympathy and encouragement, we can pass on to them this same help and comfort God has given us.

2 CORINTHIANS 1:3–4 TLB

Jesus said, "Watch out! Be very careful never to forget what you have seen God doing for you. May his miracles have a deep and permanent effect upon your lives! Tell your children and your grandchildren about the glorious miracles he did."

DEUTERONOMY 4:9 TLB

> *In the same way, faith by itself, if it is not accompanied by action, is dead.*
>
> JAMES 2:17

PRINCIPLE 8 ~ Yield myself to God to be used to bring this Good News to others, both by my example and by my words.

_____

_____

_____

_____

_____

_____

_____

_____

_____

_____

_____

_____

_____

_____

_____

_____

_____

Live and act in a way worthy of those who have been chosen
for such wonderful blessings as these.

EPHESIANS 4:1 TLB

PRINCIPLE 8 ~ Yield myself to God to be used to bring this Good News to others, both by my example and by my words.

_____

_____

_____

_____

_____

_____

_____

_____

_____

_____

_____

_____

_____

_____

_____

_____

_____

_____

_____

_____

_____

_____

_We Christians have no veil over our faces; we can be mirrors
that brightly reflect the glory of the Lord._
2 CORINTHIANS 3:18 TLB

_____

_____

_____

_____

_____

_____

_____

_____

> *In response to all he
> has done for us, let us outdo
> each other in being helpful
> and kind to each other and
> in doing good.*
>
> HEBREWS 10:24 TLB

_____

_____

_____

_____

_____

_____

_____

_____

_____

_____

> *When God's children are in need, you be the one to help them out.... Don't just pretend that you love others: really love them. Hate what is wrong. Stand on the side of the good.*
>
> ROMANS 12:13, 9 TLB

PRINCIPLE 8 ~ Yield myself to God to be used to bring this Good News to others, both by my example and by my words.

Dear brothers, if a Christian is overcome by some sin, you who are godly should gently and humbly help him back onto the right path, remembering that next time it might be one of you who is in the wrong.

GALATIANS 6:1 TLB

_____

_____

_____

_____

_____

_____

_____

_____

_____

_____

_____

_____

_____

_____

_____

_____

_____

_____

_____

*Two can accomplish more than twice as much as one, for the results can be
much better. If one falls, the other pulls him up; but if a man falls when he is
alone, he's in trouble.... And one standing alone can be attacked and defeated,
but two can stand back-to-back and conquer; three is even better,
for a triple-braided cord is not easily broken.*

ECCLESIASTES 4:9–10, 12 TLB

_____

_____

_____

_____

_____

_____

_____

> *Brothers and sisters, if someone is caught in a sin, you who live by the Spirit should restore that person gently. But watch yourself, or you also may be tempted .*
>
> GALATIANS 6:1

_____

_____

_____

_____

_____

_____

_____

_____

_____

My 90-Day Journal Review

Date _____

Search me, God, and know my heart; test me and
know my anxious thoughts. See if there is any offensive
way in me, and lead me in the way everlasting.
PSALM 139:23–24

Over the last 90 days, I can see growth in these areas:

_____

_____

_____

_____

_____

_____

_____

_____

_____

_____

_____

_____

_____

Over the last 90 days, I see that I need God to help me improve in these areas:

_____

_____

_____

_____

_____

_____

_____

_____

_____

_____

_____

_____

_____

_____

_____

_____

_____

_____

_____

_____

_____

_____

Action Plan for Growth:

_____

_____

_____

_____

_____

_____

_____

_____

_____

_____

_____

_____

_____

_____

_____

_____

_____

_____

_____

_____

_____

_____

_____

_____

_____

MY 90-DAY JOURNAL REVIEW

Date _____

Search me, God, and know my heart; test me and
know my anxious thoughts. See if there is any offensive
way in me, and lead me in the way everlasting.
PSALM 139:23–24

Over the last 90 days, I can see growth in these areas:

_____

_____

_____

_____

_____

_____

_____

_____

_____

_____

_____

_____

_____

_____

_____

Over the last 90 days, I see that I need God to help me improve in these areas:

Action Plan for Growth:

_____

_____
_____
_____
_____
_____
_____
_____
_____
_____
_____
_____
_____
_____
_____
_____
_____
_____
_____
_____
_____
_____
_____
_____
_____

MY PRAYER JOURNAL

Do not be anxious about anything, but in every situation, by prayer and petition, with thanksgiving, present your requests to God. And the peace of God, which transcends all understanding, will guard your hearts and your minds in Christ Jesus.

PHILIPPIANS 4:6–7

Date Prayed	Prayer Request (be specific)	Date Answered	God's Answer

Date Prayed	Prayer Request (be specific)	Date Answered	God's Answer

Date Prayed	Prayer Request (be specific)	Date Answered	God's Answer

Date Prayed	Prayer Request (be specific)	Date Answered	God's Answer

Date Prayed	Prayer Request (be specific)	Date Answered	God's Answer

Date Prayed	Prayer Request (be specific)	Date Answered	God's Answer

Date Prayed	Prayer Request (be specific)	Date Answered	God's Answer

Date Prayed	Prayer Request (be specific)	Date Answered	God's Answer

Date Prayed	Prayer Request (be specific)	Date Answered	God's Answer

Date Prayed	Prayer Request (be specific)	Date Answered	God's Answer

Date Prayed	Prayer Request (be specific)	Date Answered	God's Answer

Date Prayed	Prayer Request (be specific)	Date Answered	God's Answer

Celebrate Recovery Kit

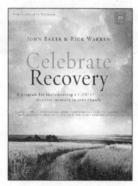

For over 25 years, *Celebrate Recovery* has helped the church fulfill its role as Christ's healing agent. Since 1991, over 1.5 million people have participated in the Celebrate Recovery programs offered at more than 29,000 churches, prisons, and rescue missions in 21 different languages. Developed by John Baker and Rick Warren of Saddleback Church, *Celebrate Recovery* draws from the Beatitudes to help people overcome their hurts, hang-ups, and habits. Rather than setting up an isolated recovery community, this powerful program helps participants and their churches come together and discover new levels of care, acceptance, trust, and grace.

Included in the 25th anniversary kit is the brand new, revolutionary step study of *The Journey Continues* which are four participant's guides that take your recovery journey deeper. The kit also includes:

- 1 leader's guide
- 1 each of *The Journey Begins* participant's guides #1–4
- 1 each of *The Journey Continues* participant's guides #5–8 (ALL NEW)
- 1 Pastor's Resource DVD with sermon transcripts, MP3 sermons, and three videos featuring John Baker, Johnny Baker, and Rick Warren
- 1 Leader's Resource DVD with 25 customizable lessons from *The Journey Begins* curriculum and three videos featuring John Baker, Johnny Baker, and Rick Warren
- 1 personal size *Celebrate Recovery Study Bible*
- 1 copy of *Your First Step to Celebrate Recovery*
- 1 copy of *Celebrate Recovery Booklet: 28 Devotions*

Available in stores and online!

ZONDERVAN®
.com